DERRICK E. BURNEY

THOSE WHO HEAR THE GOSPEL AND "[BELIEVE]" IN CHRIST

[SHOULD BE CONVINCED AND ABSOLUTELY SURE OF THEIR] "[SALVATION]"

THOSE WHO HEAR THE GOSPEL
AND "[BELIEVE]" IN CHRIST

[SHOULD BE CONVINCED AND
ABSOLUTELY SURE OF THEIR]
"[SALVATION]"

Table of Contents

INTRODUCTION

The central teaching of Christianity is the gospel, commonly referred to as the "good news." It is the announcement of Jesus Christ's death, burial, and resurrection, who died in atonement for the sins of the entire human race and rose from the grave to bring salvation and sin forgiveness to those who believe. For thousands of years, the message of the gospel has been spread over the globe. It has impacted countless lives and given those who hear and accept it hope, peace, and joy. The gospel, sometimes known as the "good news," is the core message of Christianity.

THIS BOOK WILL GIVE YOU 100% CONFIRMATION BASED ON CHRIST AND NOT YOUR WORKS EPHESIANS 2:8-9 AMP.

When You Believe In the Message, You are Saved at That Very Moment]

John 5:24 NLT

24 *"I tell you the truth, those who listen to my message and believe in God who sent me have eternal life. They will never be Condemned for Their SINS, but they have already passed from death into Life.*

According to what the Bible says, everybody who accepts the gospel of salvation through Christ is eligible for salvation. **John 5:24 NLT** proclaims this reality as follows: *[24] "I tell you the truth, those who listen to my message and believe in God who sent me have ETERNAL LIFE. They will NEVER be Condemned for their SINS, but they have already passed from Death into Life.*

This text declares that a person is saved the instant they accept the gospel of salvation via Jesus. They have transitioned from death into life and are no longer under condemnation for their transgressions. This indicates that salvation is a onetime event that occurs at the time of belief, rather than a series of events.

The gospel of redemption by faith in Christ is clear-cut and uncomplicated. It teaches that everyone has sinned and falls short of God's glory, and that sin carries a death sentence. But because God loves us so much, He sent His son, Jesus, on the cross to pay the price for our transgressions. We can get forgiveness of sins and eternal life by trusting in Jesus and His atoning work on the cross.

Everyone can benefit from this gospel of salvation through Christ, regardless of their circumstances or history. It is founded on faith in Jesus, not on our performance or capacity to uphold the law. Anyone can be saved as a result, regardless of the past, present, or future.

A person is saved and cannot lose their salvation after they have accepted the message of redemption through Jesus. Because salvation is predicated on having faith in Jesus, who cannot be lost, this is the case. Knowing that their salvation is not based on their own performance or efforts but rather on the finished work of Jesus on the cross provides believers with a sense of assurance and peace.

Accepting the gospel of redemption through Christ also results in a transformed life. This implies that when a person is rescued, their old self is killed, and they are made anew in the image of Christ. They are then able to live a brand-new life in Christ that is infused with His love, grace, and strength.

YOU WILL KNOW
[YOU ARE SAVED WITH ABSOLUTE KNOWLEDGE]

1 John 5:13 Amp

(This Is Written That You May Know ABSOLUTLY that you are SAVED)

[13] *These things I have written to you who BELIEVE in the name of the Son of God [which represents all that Jesus Christ is and does], so that you will Know [with SETTELED and ABSOLUTE Knowledge] that you [Already] Have ETERNAL LIFE.*

The Bible says that we can know for sure and without a shadow of a doubt that we are saved. I have written this to you who believe in the name of the Son of God so that you may know that you have eternal life, as stated in **1 John 5:13 AMP.**

Giving believers the certainty of their salvation is the goal of this letter, according to this verse. John wants everybody who puts their faith in the Son of God to know for certain and without a shadow of a doubt that they have eternal life. This indicates that for individuals who believe in Jesus, salvation is a settled and unquestionable reality rather than something that is ambiguous or subject to discussion.

The Holy Spirit's testimony in us is one of the most important ways we can determine whether or not we have attained salvation. When a person is saved, the Holy Spirit is given to them, and He is the one who confirms in our hearts that we are God's children.

(**Romans 8:16 AMP**). *When we place our faith in Jesus, the Holy Spirit enters our bodies and dwells there, providing us with assurance of our salvation and the certainty that we are, in fact, saved.*

The proof of changed lives is another way to know that we have been saved.

According to what the Bible teaches, when a person is saved, they are made new in Christ, and their former selves are destroyed (**2 Corinthians 5:17 Amp**).

2 Corinthians 5:17 Amp

17 Therefore if anyone is in Christ [that is, grafted in, joined to Him by faith in Him as Savior], he is a New Creature [Reborn and Renewed by the Holy Spirit]; the Old Things [the previous Moral and Spiritual Condition] HAVE PASSED AWAY. Behold, New Things have come [because Spiritual Awakening Brings a New Life].

This implies that a person's life is altered, and they are given the ability to live a life that pleases God when they are saved. The evidence of a changed life is one of the ways we can know for certain and without a doubt that we are saved. Also, it signifies that we are New Creatures which have been Reborn, Renewed and given a New Spirit by the Holy Spirits. The old sinful spirit has been ripped out of us and buried by the Holy Spirit. Understanding this New development from God gives you a whole New Life.

One further method by which we can be certain we are saved is by our adherence to God's word. The Bible asserts that individuals who are actually saved will carry out God's instructions (**1 John 2:3-6 Amp**). We demonstrate our love for God and our status as His children when we obey His word. This obedience serves as a sign of our salvation and a testament to it.

The joy and serenity that come from having a connection with Jesus are also signs that we are saved. According to what the Bible teaches, once we are saved, we are at peace with God, and nothing can ever take that away from us (**Romans 8:38– 39 Amp**).

Finally, the Bible teaches us that we can be certain of and satisfied with our salvation. This knowledge is gained through the Holy Spirit's witness, the proof of changed lives, our obedient living according to God's word, and the peace and joy that result from having a personal relationship with Jesus. We can live with assurance and delight knowing that we are God's children and that we have eternal life when we have this firm and unwavering understanding of our salvation.

IF YOU BELIEVE YOU HAVE DIVINE PUNISHMENT FOR YOUR SINS AFTER YOU HAVE ACCEPTED CHRIST, YOU DO NOT HAVE A PROPER UNDERSTANDING OF GOD'S LOVE.

1 John 4:16-18 Amp

(If you have a fear of divine punishment from God? Then you do not understand God's perfect Love for you.)

16 We have come to know [by personal observation and experience], and have believed [with deep, consistent faith] the love which God has for us. God is love, and the one who abides in love abides in God, and God abides continually in him. 17 In this [union and fellowship with Him], love is completed and perfected with us, so that we may have confidence in the day of judgment [with assurance and boldness to face Him]; because as He is, so are we in this world.

*¹⁸ There is no fear in love [dread does not exist]. But perfect (complete, full-grown) love drives out fear, because fear involves [the expectation of divine] punishment, **so the one who is afraid [of God's judgment]** is Not Perfected in LOVE [**has not grown into a sufficient understanding of God's LOVE**].*

Even if they trust in God's love, many people who have accepted Christ as their Savior nevertheless suffer with the fear of eternal retribution. However, it shows that you do not have a sufficient grasp of God's love if you think that you will experience divine punishment after embracing Christ.

In 1 John 4:16–18, which is translated in the New Living Translation (NLT), the Bible instructs us on how to understand and rely on God's love for us. It says, "And so we know and rely on the love God has for us." God is love. Anyone who lives in love lives in God, and God lives in them. "This is how love is made complete among us so that we will have confidence on the Day of Judgment: in this world, we are like Jesus."

According to this scripture, God is love, and anyone who lives in love is both a part of God and a part of God. This translates to us receiving God's love into our hearts when we embrace Jesus as our Savior. On the Day of Judgment, we will have confidence if we live in that love.

It reads, "In the Amplified Version." "And we've learned to understand and accept God's love for us." He who abides in love abides in God, and God abides in him. God is love. As a result, love is perfected in our relationship, giving us hope for the Day of Judgment because, like Him, we exist in this world.

According to this verse, when we live in love, we abide in God, and when we dwell in God, we have faith on the day of judgment. This implies that we do not need to be afraid of divine punishment if we have received Christ as our Savior and are acting in love.

In summary, if you think that adopting Christ will subject you to divine retribution, it indicates that your understanding of God's love is flawed. God is love, and when we practice loving kindness in our daily lives, we stay connected to God and have faith in the coming Day of Judgment. Therefore, if you are a follower of Christ, do not fear eternal punishment but rather put your faith in God's love and practice living in love, knowing that you are in the right standing with God.

CHAPTER ONE

WHY SHOULD WE BE ABSOLUTELY CERTAIN OF OUR SALVATION?

Lesson Objective

At the end of this module, you should be able to understand the following:

- Why should we have absolute certainty about our salvation?

- What happened to your sin?

- Make it clear that Christ is proclaiming your sins are forgiven.

- We are declared free from the guilt of sin and thereby saved from the consequences of sin by Christ's life.

- God was reconciling the world to himself through Christ, restoring him to God's favor.

- No more consciousness of sin

- (Believe in Jesus and your name will never be looted out of the book of life.)

Whether or not one will be saved after death is one of the most fundamental and significant issues that one can ask oneself. Because it gives us a sense of confidence and comfort in knowing that our fate is assured, the idea of perfect assurance of our salvation appeals to us.

We should seek complete assurance of our salvation for a number of reasons. First off, it makes life more meaningful and purposeful for us. When we are sure of our salvation, we may concentrate our efforts on leading a life that is honoring to God and helpful to others. This gives us a sense of direction and enables us to stay away from the world's temptations and diversions.

Second, having complete assurance of our salvation provides us comfort and hope when faced with difficulties. We can confront the challenges of life with courage and resiliency when we are confident that our fate is secure. In times of bereavement, illness, or other difficulties when we might feel overwhelmed and unclear about the future, this might be especially crucial.

Thirdly, having complete assurance of our salvation encourages us to provide more mercy and compassion to others. Knowing that we have been saved enables us to treat people with kindness and empathy, even when they mistreat us or cause us harm. This can improve social cohesion and harmony while also strengthening our interpersonal bonds.

Fourth, having complete assurance of our salvation might aid us in avoiding sin and temptation. We are less likely to be misled by worldly demands and temptations and more likely to remain steadfast in our faith and commitment to God when we are confident that our fate is secure.

In conclusion, there are a number of strong arguments for why we should work toward complete assurance of our salvation. Having complete assurance of our salvation is a worthwhile goal for all of us to strive for, whether it is for a more meaningful and purposeful life, greater hope and peace in the face of adversity, greater compassion and forgiveness toward others, or greater resistance to temptation and sin. It is crucial to keep in mind that, despite the fact that we are unable to obtain complete certainty on our own, we can strengthen our relationship with God by praying, giving thanks, and obeying his commands. As we do so, our assurance of salvation will become stronger, giving us more comfort and security in both this life and the next.

WHAT HAPPENED TO YOUR SINS?

(It Is By God's Grace You Have Been Delivered From Sin, Not By Works Of Your Own; It's An Undeserved Gift.)

(Ephesians 2:8–9 AMP) from the Amplified Bible says, "For it is by grace [God's remarkable compassion and favor drawing you to Christ] that you have been saved [actually delivered from judgment and given eternal life] through faith." "And this [salvation] is not of yourselves [not through your own effort], but it is the gift of God; not as a result of works [not the fulfillment of the law's demands], so that no one may boast."

These words emphasize that salvation and sin forgiveness are gifts from God that are obtained through faith in Jesus Christ rather than through deeds or human effort. In other words, we are saved and have our sins forgiven only through God's grace. This thought is in line with the Christian doctrine that salvation is a free gift from God and that the only way to be at peace with God and get forgiveness for our sins is by placing our confidence in Jesus.

Therefore, God's grace and our faith in Jesus Christ—rather than our deeds or efforts—determine the outcome of our sins. Our sins are pardoned, we are delivered from judgment, and we are given eternal life when we trust in Jesus as our Savior.

The fact that we have placed our trust in Jesus and are saved by God's grace should not be used to imply that we will never sin again. Christians still battle with sin on a daily basis, but thanks to salvation, they have a way to be forgiven and repair their connection with God when they do.

In *1 John 1:9,* it says, *"If we confess our sins, He is faithful and just to forgive us our sins and to cleanse us from all unrighteousness." This verse emphasizes the importance of confessing our sins to God and relying on his forgiveness. When we confess our sins, we acknowledge our wrongdoing and ask for God's forgiveness. God, in his faithfulness and justice, is always ready to forgive and cleanse us from our unrighteousness.*

In conclusion, God's grace and our faith in Jesus Christ determine what happens to our sins. Our sins are covered by salvation, and we are guaranteed an eternity with God. Even if we still battle sin on a daily basis, we can count on God's mercy when we repent and seek his guidance. We can have the confidence and peace of knowing that our sins are forgiven and that we have a new life in him through having faith in Jesus and depending on God's grace.

MAKE IT CLEAR: CHRIST IS CLAIMING YOUR SINS ARE FORGIVEN.

(Acts 13:38–39) from the Amplified Bible says, "Therefore, my brethren, I declare to you, through Him [Jesus], everyone who believes [who adheres to, trusts in, and relies on Him] is absolved (declared righteous and freed) from his

sins. Be careful to pay attention to these things, because it is through Him [your obedience] that you will receive full and fair forgiveness of your sins and right standing with God.

These lines make it very apparent that it is only through Jesus that we are justified and set free from our sins. The text underlines that trusting in and following Jesus will result in forgiveness. The forgiveness that restores our right standing with God is complete and just.

This verse emphasizes how crucial faith in and submission to Jesus are for atonement. It makes it abundantly clear that there is no other way to be pardoned of our sins but by placing our faith in Jesus. We can enjoy the confidence and peace of knowing that our sins are forgiven and that we have a new life in him by putting our trust in him and adhering to his teachings.

Christ Life Saves Us From The Consequences Of Sin. Because We Are Declared Free From The Guilt Of Sin.

(Romans 5:9–10) from the Amplified Bible says, "Much more then, since we have now been declared righteous as a result of faith, let us seize the opportunity to experience peace with God and the joy of His salvation." This can be ours through faith. "For we have become united with Him in His death through our baptism, in order that just as Christ was raised from the dead by the glorious [power] of the Father, so we too might [habitually] live and behave in the newness of life [abstractly, in a new sphere of life and being]."

These lines stress that we have been justified by faith and delivered from the penalty of sin. The joy of God's salvation and peace with him are made possible by this proclamation of righteousness. Because of our belief in Jesus, we share in his death, and because of his resurrection, we are also able to live and act in a way that is consistent with new life.

This verse emphasizes how having trust in Jesus may change your life and give you knew life. It emphasizes that we are delivered from the guilt of sin and protected from its repercussions through trust in Jesus. By placing our faith in Jesus, we can have confidence and security in knowing that we have a new life in him, free from the guilt and repercussions of sin.

NO MORE CONSCIOUSNESS OF SIN

(Hebrews 10:2) from the Amplified Bible says, "Otherwise, would [these sacrifices] not have stopped being offered?" "For the worshipers would have been cleansed once for all and would no longer have felt guilty for their sins."

This passage focuses on the fact that the worshipers were cleansed and no longer felt sorry for their sins as a result of the offerings made under the old covenant. This emphasizes the transitory and constrained nature of previous sacrifices and emphasizes the want for a superior sacrifice that would offer a long-lasting remedy for sin.

This line can be interpreted as a preview of Jesus' ultimate sacrifice, which is his death on the cross, which offers a long-lasting remedy for sin. By placing our faith in Jesus, we can have confidence and security in knowing that our sins are forgiven and that we no longer have to live with the guilt of sin.

Hebrews 10:2 emphasizes the supremacy of Jesus' sacrifice above the transient and constrained offerings of the previous covenant in this way. It makes it obvious that we can be forgiven of our sins and freed from the burden of guilt by placing our faith in Jesus. Our assurance and security in a brand-new existence in him, free from sin and its repercussions, are provided by this.

One of the most priceless gifts we may receive is the forgiveness of sins through faith in Jesus, which is a basic tenet of the Christian religion. It puts us in God's good graces and provides us the peace of mind that comes from knowing we have a new life in him. As we develop in our faith and follow Jesus more closely, we continually experience this forgiveness.

Our style of life changes when we have complete assurance of our salvation. It liberates us from the shame and guilt of our sin and gives us the courage to live a courageous life for Christ. We may now fully experience the joy and serenity that come from knowing that our sins are forgiven and that we have a new life in Jesus, rather than having to live in terror of the repercussions of our wrongdoing.

To sum up, having complete assurance of our salvation is crucial for our spiritual development and wellbeing. It gives us the comfort and peace of knowing that we have a new life in Jesus and that our sins have been forgiven. The freedom it gives us to live freely for Christ and to enjoy the fullness of joy and peace that come from knowing that our salvation is secure affects the way we live.

God Was In Christ Not Counting Our Sins Against Us.

(2 Corinthians 5:19–22) the Amplified Bible says, "It was God [personally present] in Christ, Not Counting People's SINS AGAINST THEM HE WAS CANCELING THEM. HE WAS RECONCILING and restoring the world BACK to favor with Himself, not counting up and holding SINS against [men] and their trespasses [but canceling them], and committing to us the message of

reconciliation (of the restoration to favor). So we are Christ's representatives, God appealing to you as we speak on

On his behalf; we beg you, as if Christ Himself were present, to be reconciled to God. For our sake, He made Christ [virtually] sin who knew no sin, that we might become [endued with, viewed as being in, and examples of] God's righteousness

[what we ought to be, approved and acceptable, and in right relationship with Him, by His goodness] in and through Him.

The crucial role that Jesus plays in God's plan of rapprochement is emphasized in this text. It emphasizes that God himself was present in Christ, bringing about the world's reconciliation with him and regaining his favor. By not Counting their SINS AGAINST THEM. GOD achieved this reconciliation by erasing and not holding the sins of men against them.

Through this reconciliation, we are transformed into Christ's representatives, asking for others to experience God's reconciliation with them. This verse emphasizes how Jesus, who was without sin, became sin for us so that, through him, we might attain the righteousness of God.

In this way, **2 Corinthians 5:19–21 Amp** emphasizes the sacrifice of Jesus and the new life it gives, as well as its ability to transform. It clearly states that we are made right with God and restored to his favor through our belief in Jesus. This provides us the confidence and security of a brand-new life in him, one that is devoid of sin and its negative effects and filled with God's righteousness.

Believe In Jesus And Your Name

Will Never Be Taken Out Of The Book Of Life.

(Revelation 3:5) in the Amplified Bible says, "He who is victorious shall thus be clothed in white garments, and I will not erase or blot out his name from the book of life; I will acknowledge him [as mine] and confess his name before My Father and before His angels."

This text alludes to the "book of life," which is a metaphor for God's record of every person who has ever lived. When a person trusts in Jesus and is saved, the Bible says that their name is recorded in the book of life. According to this scripture, no one's name will ever be removed from the book of life provided they persevere in their faith, which is understood to entail believing in Jesus.

This is how Revelation 3:5 gives us a strong assurance of our salvation and the peace of mind that comes from knowing that our names are recorded in the book of life. It is a reassuring reminder that we are saved and have a permanent home in heaven. Knowing that our future is safe and that our name will never be removed from the book of life gives us the courage to live bravely for Christ.

Having the certainty of our salvation via faith in Jesus, then, is a crucial component of our faith. The assurance that our names will never be removed from the Book of Life is a potent illustration of the secure and enduring nature of our salvation. It gives us the assurance to live courageously for Christ, knowing that our salvation is an unchangeable, everlasting truth.

CHAPTER TWO

"OVERCOME THE WORLD."
WHAT IS OVERCOMING THE WORLD?

Lesson objective

At the end of this module, you should be able to understand the following:

+ "Overcome the world." What is overcoming the world?

+ Who is the one the Bible considers to have overcome the world?

+ Overcoming the world is what happens when you believe in Jesus.

+ Furthermore, God holds the key to your salvation, and he has stated that nothing he has created can take it away from you.

+ They have refused to accept God's righteousness, instead attempting to establish their own.

+ Nothing can separate us from God's Love.

The idea of "overcoming the world" alludes to success in the face of life's many hardships, challenges, and hurdles. This can range from local issues like poverty or environmental degradation to global issues like low self-esteem or despair. To overcome the world, one must rise above these challenges and discover a method to win despite them.

For many people, conquering the world begins with a shift in perspective. We must shift our attention from what is wrong or what is preventing us to what is achievable and what we can do to overcome the problems before us. This calls for optimism and self-confidence, despite what may appear to be insurmountable obstacles and the RENEWING OF YOUR MIND.

One strategy for overcoming the world is to develop a strong sense of self-awareness IN CHRIST and work to better us from a SPIRITUAL PERSPECTIVE FROM GOD'S RIGHTEOUSNESS and GRACE developed from the inside out. We can create a stronger feeling of self-confidence and resilience by becoming more aware of our New Spiritual condition in Christ 2 Corinthian's 5:17 Amp. This will enable us to address the obstacles we face head-on Spiritually.

Believing in Christ is a crucial part of overcoming the world. We can conquer even the most difficult challenges and make our aspirations come true by acting consistently and persistently accepting tge work Christ has done for us.

Making a difference in the world is an important part of many people's definitions of "overcoming the world." This can entail helping others through volunteering, contributing to philanthropic causes, or trying to improve their circumstances. We can improve the world by helping others, but we can also deepen our own sense of meaning and purpose by doing so. But Most Importantly our position to the World is being Ambassadors for

Christ. Which is Telling the World their Sins Are Completely forgiven by Christ and in Christ. Which brings Salvation and them back to FAVOR with God 2 Corinthians 5:19-21 Amp.

It is not always simple to overcome the world, and there will be instances when we may feel helpless or discouraged. But it's crucial to keep in mind that failing is a normal part of the process and that making mistakes is acceptable. Instead of giving up, we must get back up, acknowledge our errors, and continue moving forward in Christ.

In the end, conquering the world is about acquiring the fortitude, bravery, and resiliency to meet problems head-on through the Holy Spirit. It is about discovering the inner strength to overcome the challenges and hardships we encounter and to build a rich, purposeful life in and for Christ.

Ultimately, overcoming the world is a voyage of personal development, expansion, and transformation. It calls for a positive outlook, a strong sense of self-awareness, regular action, and a dedication to having a beneficial influence on the world by believing in the work Christ has done for you.

John 6:28

28 Then they asked Him, "What are we to do, so that we may habitually be doing the works of God?" Jesus answered,

29 "This is the work of God: that you BELIEVE [adhere to, trust in, rely on, AND have Faith] in the One whom He has sent."

We may triumph over the world and build a life that is genuinely rich and happy by accepting this journey and BELIVING IN THE WORK CHRIST DID FOR US

Who Is Believed By The Bible To Have Overcome The World.?

According to the Bible, Jesus Christ is regarded as having triumphed over the world. In (**John 16:33**), Jesus makes this claim: *"I told you these things so you could find comfort in me." You will face difficulties in this life. But have courage!*

"I've Overcome the World!" Jesus' victory over sin and death through his death and resurrection is what causes people to believe that he has conquered the world. His sacrifice on the cross eventually overcame the authority of sin and death. He encountered great difficulties and temptations, but he stayed obedient to God's will.

Jesus gives those who place their faith in him hope and redemption by triumphing over the world. He demonstrated to us that it is possible to hold fast and find comfort and delight in God even in the midst of the most difficult trials. We can conquer the world and achieve freedom from our problems, fears, and anxieties by following Jesus.

In this way, Jesus is viewed as a role model for how we might conquer the world as well. We can discover the courage to meet life's obstacles and experience the peace and joy that come from a life rooted in God by having confidence in him and by imitating his behavior.

You Overcome the World When You Believe In Jesus.

According to the Bible, overcoming the world happens when we believe in Jesus. In (**1 John 5:4–5 AMP**), it states: *"For everyone who has been born of God overcomes the world." And this is the victory that has overcome the world— our faith. "Who is it that overcomes the world except the one who believes that Jesus is the Son of God?"*

To put it another way, we are equipped to triumph over the world and all of its troubles, obstacles, and temptations because we believe that Jesus is the Son of God. We are given the power and grace to remain steadfast and get through life's challenges when we place our confidence in Jesus.

This chapter emphasizes the crucial role that faith plays in prevailing over the world. When the world is turbulent, our faith in Jesus provides us the strength and assurance to face life's problems and hold fast to our convictions.

So, according to the Bible, putting our faith and trust in Jesus to lead and empower us is the secret to overcoming the world. By doing this, we can enjoy the triumph and serenity that come from living in God's power and grace.

We have a stronger sense of hope and purpose when we believe in Jesus and trust in his ability to defeat the world. Knowing that Jesus is always by our side and directing us allows us to find calm in the midst of the upheaval and turbulence of the world.

Furthermore, by placing our confidence in Jesus, we can have the direction and discernment we require to face life's obstacles and make choices that are in line with God's purpose. Because we are no longer controlled by fear or anxiety but rather are energized by a strong sense of purpose and direction, this can help us live a more satisfying and meaningful life.

To sum up, it takes faith in Jesus and confidence in his ability to lead and empower us to overcome the world. We may rely on him to give us the courage, serenity, and insight we require to meet life's problems and build meaningful, purposeful lives. We can triumph over the world and enjoy the victory that comes from abiding in God's strength and grace through faith in Jesus.

Because God has the Power To Save You; He Stated, Nothing He Has Ever Created Can Snatch You From His Hands.

This is a crucial Christian truth that gives those who accept Jesus Christ as their Savior a wonderful sense of relief and calm. According to the Bible, God is the source of our salvation and has promised that nothing will be able to take it away from us. As a result, we may rest assured that our salvation is safe and that it won't be snatched from us.

In (**Romans 8:38–39**), the apostle Paul stated, "*38 For I am convinced [and continue to be convinced—beyond any doubt] that neither death, nor life, nor angels, nor principalities, nor things present and threatening, nor things to come, nor powers,*

39 nor height, nor depth, nor any other created thing, will be able to separate us from the [unlimited] love of God, which is in Christ Jesus our Lord"

This chapter reminds us that nothing in this life, heaven, or hell can take our salvation away from us, giving us a strong confidence in it.

Our assurance of salvation is a gift of God's grace and love; it is unrelated to anything we are or have done. Our salvation is not dependent on how well we do or how well we can uphold it. Neither can we earn it or deserve it. Our salvation is a free gift from God that cannot be reversed and is totally dependent on our faith in Jesus Christ.

The effectiveness of God's salvation also applies to our earthly lives as well as our eternal ones. When we place our faith in Jesus, the Holy Spirit works inside us to transform us and give us the capacity to live godly lives. We have the ability to triumph over sin and lead liberated lives. In addition, we are given the assurance that God will be with us and assist us as we face life's obstacles.

In conclusion, it's crucial to keep in mind that God alone possesses the ability to bring about our salvation and that He has promised that nothing will be able to revoke it from us. Our assurance of salvation rests exclusively on our faith in Jesus Christ. May we never lose sight of the fact that God alone holds the key to our salvation and that nothing can take it away from us ever. Because for us to lose our Salvation they would have to TAKE IT FROM GOD FIRST. And he has promised us that NOTHING CAN PULL US OUT OF HIS HANDS. May we always be confident in our SALVATION as well as in GOD'S LOVE and GRACE TO HOLD OUR SALVATION IN HIS HANDS.

They Have Not Accepted God's Righteousness

The apostle Paul stated in (**Romans 10:3–4),** *"Because they are unaware of God's Righteousness and are attempting to uphold their own righteousness, they have not yielded to God's righteousness." "For Christ is the END of the Law for Righteousness for Everyone that BELIEVES in him as Savior."* This verse emphasizes how crucial it is to submit to God's righteousness rather than seeking to build our own.

Many individuals, including Jews in Paul's day, frequently attempt to prove their own righteousness through adherence to the Torah or reliance on their own valiant deeds. However, the Bible teaches that our own righteousness is worthless in God's eyes and that we are unable to earn God's favor on our own. Faith in Jesus Christ, who fulfilled the law for us and died on the cross to pay the price for our sin, is the only way to be reconciled to God.

When we acknowledge God's righteousness, we stop striving to earn God's favor and start depending on His compassion and mercy to save us. We are placing our faith in the righteousness of Jesus Christ, which has been credited to us, rather than seeking to establish our own righteousness. This permits us to relax in the knowledge that we are saved by grace through faith in Jesus Christ and releases us from the pressure of attempting to earn God's favor.

Additionally, we are given the ability to live a decent life when we accept God's righteousness. We are transformed by the Holy Spirit, who also empowers us to live godly lives. Because we have abundantly benefited from God's love and grace, we are also able to be kind and compassionate toward others.

In conclusion, a crucial component of our faith in Jesus Christ is accepting God's righteousness. Through faith in Jesus Christ, we can be saved by grace because we cannot make peace with God on our own. May we never forget that our righteousness is derived from the atonement made by Jesus on the cross? Instead, may we never seek to build our own righteousness?

(NOTHING CAN SEPARATE US FROM OUR SALVATION IN CHRIST.)

In (**Romans 8:33–39 Amp**), the apostle Paul wrote,

33*"Who shall bring a charge against God's elect?" It is God who justifies. Who is he who condemns? It is Christ who died and, furthermore, is also raised, who is even at the right hand of God, who also makes intercession for us. Who will separate us from the love of Christ? Should there be tribulation, distress, persecution, famine, nakedness, peril, or sword?*

38*For I am convinced [and continue to be convinced—beyond any doubt] that neither death, nor life, nor angels, nor principalities, nor things present and threatening, nor things to come, nor powers,*

39*nor height, nor depth, nor any other created thing, will be able to separate us from the [unlimited] love of God, which is in Christ Jesus our Lord.*

This text gives us a lot of hope and comfort by reassuring us that nothing can separate us from Christ's love. We are never alone in life's challenges, whether they are trials, suffering, persecution, or any other type of adversity, since the love of Christ is always with us.

The verse also teaches us that because Christ loved us and offered Himself for us, we are more than conquerors. In other words, despite the problems and difficulties we may encounter in life, we are able to overcome them because of our faith in

Jesus Christ. The things that happen to us do not defeat us; rather, the strength of Christ empowers us to triumph.

The scripture also serves as a reminder that Christ is at God's right hand, making pleas on our behalf, and that it is God who justifies us. This provides us with the comfort of knowing that we are constantly in the presence of a loving and caring God who is acting in our best interests.

In conclusion, it is a strong and uplifting fact for believers to know that nothing can separate us from Christ's love. We can always have faith that the love of Christ is with us and that, because of Him, we are victorious over all that we encounter in life. Because nothing will ever be able to separate us from Christ's love, may we always hold fast to this truth and never lose sight of the fact that we are never alone.

SALVATION

Lesson objective

At the end of this module, you should be able to understand the following:

- The Definition of Salvation

- Scriptural references to salvation in the Amplified Bible

- No More Consciousness of Sin

- (Believe in Jesus; your name will never be tossed out of the book of life.)

THE DEFINITION OF SALVATION

The act of being rescued, redeemed, and delivered from sin and its consequences by trusting in Jesus Christ is known as salvation, and it is a key idea in Christianity. According to what the Bible says, Jesus Christ's death and resurrection made it possible for people to receive salvation as a gift from God.

The Christian faith holds that salvation is necessary since all people are sinners by nature and fall short of God's ideal. Without redemption, people are cut off from

God and sentenced to an eternity of torment in Hell. However, a person can be spared from this fate and made right with God by placing their faith in Jesus Christ.

Christianity bases salvation on the idea that God in the flesh, Jesus Christ, died on the cross to atone for humankind's sins. This act of self-giving atoned for sin and offered a pathway for others to find forgiveness and peace with God. A person can be given the gift of salvation and transformed by the power of the Holy Spirit by confessing Jesus Christ as Lord and Savior.

A person must acknowledge their sins, turn from them, and put their faith in Jesus Christ in order to be saved. This entails admitting their sinfulness, abstaining from sin, and fully putting their faith in Jesus as the only way to be saved. It involves a commitment to follow Jesus and live in accordance with His teachings, which is a personal choice.

Christian salvation is dependent on God's grace alone, not on human merit or good deeds. This indicates that it is a gift given to those who believe, rather than something that can be acquired or earned. It is crucial to understand that salvation is a process that starts with the initial act of faith and lasts the rest of a person's life as they develop a closer connection with God and more closely resemble Jesus.

The forgiveness of sins is one of the advantages of salvation. A person's sins are pardoned, and they are reconciled to God through trust in Jesus. Individuals experience serenity and a fresh relationship with God as a result of this forgiveness. Salvation also results in a change of heart, enabling people to live a holy and blameless life and grow more in the likeness of Jesus.

The assurance of eternal life is another facet of salvation. According to what the Bible says, individuals who are saved will spend all of eternity in heaven with God, basking in His glory and experiencing the depths of His love. People who are looking for significance and hope in a world that can often be depressing will find this to be a compelling and uplifting message.

Salvation means rescuing from danger. As I realized the preacher was telling us to "be saved," the word made more sense. Salvation usually means being saved from sin by God. But, the Bible describes salvation as more than escaping damnation.

It's helpful to consider salvation from, to, and by. See salvation as a past, present, and future event.

We are Saved from our real problem sin through Jesus Christ. "Sin and guilt are at the root of the problem. Because of this, there is a problem. Since we are all sinners, it was necessary for God to send Jesus Christ as a savior to save us from hell. You are a sinner whether you are rich or poor, hopeful or pessimistic, given over to your desires or able to exercise some self-control and discipline. God is very displeased with you because you have disobeyed His commandment. If your current situation doesn't improve, you're doomed to spend eternity in hell. You are in desperate need of deliverance from the penalties of your sin. The gospel provides answers to those core problems."

Who Saves us from the death sentence? God is the one who enacts Salvation. The Scriptures are clear that the way of unbelief is to trust in self or in other things for salvation. Psalms 20 nkjv shows that the way of belief is to not trust in chariots or horses but to trust in the name of the Lord. We are the ones who have gotten ourselves into the mess; therefore God alone is able to saves(1Timothy 1:15 Amp) is clear that Jesus came into the world to save sinners. This means every sinner, if he/she is to be saved will be saved through BELIEVING IN CHRIST as Savior.

What Are We Saved For? We have been preserved for a romantic connection a real relationship with God.. God has triumphed over our most difficult challenges in order to make it possible for us to have a relationship with him. This is the most important benefit for us. But how exactly do we get ownership of this? Is there no one who will not be saved as a result of what Christ has done?

Last but not least, salvation is a key and foundational idea in Christianity. By being saved, redeemed, and freed from sin and its effects via faith in Jesus Christ, one is said to be doing these things. It is a gift from God that necessitates a conscious choice to acknowledge sin, turn from it, and put your confidence in Jesus. Forgiveness, transformation, and the assurance of an eternity with God in paradise are all advantages of salvation.

The significance of comprehending salvation within the context of the gospel

It is essential to comprehend what salvation means in the context of the gospel since it is essential to the Christian message. Salvation is the state of being delivered from sin and death, as well as the mending of the conflict between humanity and God.

The good news is that people can be saved by having faith in Jesus Christ and His atoning death and resurrection. According to the Bible, sin has caused a gap between humanity and God, and salvation fills that gap. In this view, salvation is a whole idea that embraces both the transformation of a believer's life by the power of the Holy Spirit and the forgiveness of sins.

Therefore, having a clear knowledge of what salvation entails can aid believers in deepening their faith, leading God-honoring lives, and sharing the gospel with others in a powerful way. It also aids in preventing misunderstandings or false beliefs about salvation and its goal.

In conclusion, comprehending what salvation entails within the framework of the gospel is critical for one's own spiritual development, an effective witness, and a greater understanding of God's grace and love.

Scriptures Reference to Salvation In The Bible

(John 3:16 Amp): *"For God so greatly loved and dearly prized the world that He [even] gave up His only begotten (unique) Son, so that whoever believes in (trusts in, clings to, relies on) Him shall not perish (come to destruction, be lost) but have eternal (everlasting) life."*

(**Romans 10:9–10**): *"If you confess with your mouth that Jesus is Lord and believe in your heart that God raised him from the dead, you will be saved." "For with the heart one believes (adheres to, trusts in, and relies on Christ) and thus is justified (declared righteous, acceptable to God), and with the mouth one confesses (declares openly and freely his faith) and is saved."*

Ephesians 2:8-9 AMP

8 For it is by grace [God's remarkable compassion and favor drawing you to Christ] that you have been saved [actually delivered from judgment and given eternal life] through faith. 9 And this [salvation] is not of yourselves [not through your own effort], but it is the [undeserved, gracious] gift of God; not as a result of [your] works [nor your attempts to keep the Law], so that no one will [be able to] boast or take credit in any way [for his salvation].

John 5:24 NLT

24"I tell you the truth, those who listen to my message and believe in God who sent me have eternal life. They will never be condemned for their sins, but they have already passed from death into life.

Revelation 3:5 AMP

*⁵ He who overcomes [the world through believing that Jesus is the Son of God] will accordingly be dressed in white clothing; and **I will never blot out his name from the Book of Life,** and I will confess and openly acknowledge his name before My Father and before His angels [saying that he is one of Mine].*

NO MORE CONSCIOUSNESS OF SIN

(**Hebrews 10:2 AMP**) Hebrews 10:2 (AMP)

2 For if it were otherwise, would not these sacrifices have stopped being offered? For the worshipers, having once [for all time] been cleansed, would no longer have a consciousness of sin. **because they had been cleansed once [FOR ALL TIME].**

God Was In Christ Not Counting Your Sin's Against You.

God reconciled the world to Himself through Christ, NOT COUNTING PEOPLE'S SINS AGAINST THEM [but CANCELING THEM] (2 Corinthians 5:19-21 AMP). 2 Corinthians 5:19

[19] *that is, that God was in Christ reconciling the world to Himself, not counting people's sins against them [but canceling them]. And He has committed to us the message of reconciliation [that is, restoration to favor with God].* [20] *So we are ambassadors for Christ, as though God were making His appeal through us; we [as Christ's representatives] plead with you on behalf of Christ to be reconciled to God.* [21] *He made Christ who knew no sin to [judicially] be sin on our behalf, so that in Him we would become the righteousness of God [that is, we would be made acceptable to Him and placed in a right relationship with Him by His gracious lovingkindness].*

Believe In Jesus And Your Name
Will Never Be Blotted Out The Book Of Life.

(Revelation 3:5 AMP) He who overcomes [the world through believing that Jesus is the Son of God] will accordingly be dressed in white clothing, and I will NEVER BLOT OUT HIS NAME from the Book of Life, and I will confess and openly acknowledge his name before My Father and before His angels [saying that he is one of mine].

"OVERCOME THE WORLD":
WHAT IS OVERCOMING THE WORLD SPIRITUALLY?

Lesson objective

At the end of this module, you should be able to understand the following: "Overcome the World": What is Overcoming the World?

Who Is the One the Bible Considers has Overcome The World.?

I John 5:4–5 AMP of the Bible describes a person who has triumphed over the world: "Because everything that comes from God triumphs over the material world and our faith is the source of this victory." "Who else but the person who has faith in Jesus as the Son of God overcomes the world?" This verse makes it quite apparent that the one who has triumphed over the world is one who is a child of God and believes that Jesus is the Son of God.

The idea of conquering the earth is essential to the Christian faith because it symbolizes victory over sin, mortality, and the devil. The world is frequently represented in the Bible as the powers of evil and those who oppose God. These forces aim to draw individuals away from God and His truth in a variety of ways, including temptation, opposition, and deceptive teaching.

However, the Bible teaches that believers can triumph over the world and its difficulties by placing their confidence in Jesus Christ. This is due to the fact that, through His death and resurrection, Jesus Himself defeated the world. By defeating sin, death, and the devil, He also made it possible for believers to triumph over these same forces.

Believers are given a new spiritual nature that is in harmony with God when they come to faith in Jesus. Because of their new nature, they are able to overcome the world's obstacles. In other words, believers have access to God's power through faith in Jesus, which enables them to live triumphant lives.

The Bible also teaches that having faith in Jesus changes how a person sees the world. Believers are able to view events from God's perspective and recognize that the things of this world are fleeting, rather than focusing on the transient things of this world. As Jesus said in **John 17:14–16,** this new viewpoint enables believers to live in the world without becoming a part of it.

In conclusion, the person who has overcome the world according to the Bible is one who has been born of God by accepting Jesus Christ as the Son of God. This individual is able to overcome sin, death, and the devil because they have access to God's strength and a fresh outlook on the world. All who place their faith in Jesus will experience this victory because of His death and resurrection.

Christ Put You In Right Standing With God.

Lesson objective

Your belief in Christ as Savior, puts you in Right Standing with God.

According to what the Bible says anybody who accepts Jesus Christ as their personal Savior can be persuaded that they are saved and in good standing with God. Romans 10:3–4 AMP makes this plain when it says, "Because the Jews strove to establish their own righteousness and refused to submit to

God's righteousness, they were unaware of the righteousness that God [by His grace] made accessible to them." "Because the law of righteousness has been fulfilled in him for anyone who believes in Christ as Savior."

Jesus' death and resurrection resulted in the righteousness that God offers to Christians. Believers get God's righteousness and forgiveness for their sins by placing their faith in Jesus. This indicates that they are in good standing with God and that they are no longer cut off from Him. They can be assured that they are saved and will have eternal life as a result.

The Bible also says that in order to be saved, one must accept Jesus as their personal Savior. Romans 10:9–10 (AMP) reads, "Because you will be saved if you publicly profess with your mouth that Jesus is Lord and firmly believe in your heart that God actually did raise him from the dead." "Because a person's confidence in Jesus as the Christ is expressed via both their heart and their words, resulting in righteousness and salvation, respectively,"

The necessity of accepting Jesus as your personal Savior is made very apparent in this verse. It is insufficient to merely be aware of Jesus or to hold a religious conviction about Him. Instead, genuine belief entails praising Jesus as Lord and trusting in His Crucifixion and Resurrection.

Additionally, the Bible teaches that accepting Jesus as Savior causes Christians' lives to change. Through faith in Jesus, believers are given a new spiritual nature that is in harmony with God. They are able to live godly lives and receive all of God's gifts thanks to their new nature.

Believers' outlook on life is changed by accepting Jesus as their Savior. They now see themselves as God's children with the possibility of eternal life rather than as captives to sin and death. They are now able to approach life's obstacles with joy and assurance because they now understand how much God loves and cares for them.

Finally, having a close relationship with God is a result of accepting Jesus as your Savior. According to what the Bible says, people can approach the Father and encounter His love and grace by placing their confidence in Jesus. Additionally, they are able to develop a close relationship with the Holy Spirit, who serves as their personal guide and source of strength.

In summary, the Bible teaches that those who accept Jesus Christ as their Savior can be persuaded that they are saved and in good standing with God. The fullness of God's blessings, a fresh outlook on life, and a strong relationship with God are just a few of the changes that result from this conviction, which is necessary for salvation.

CONCLUSION

Finally, those who hear the gospel should be confident that they have been saved. The Bible gives explicit instructions on this subject, declaring that you are saved if you confess Jesus as your Lord and Savior. Your heart should feel assured and at ease as a result of this belief.

Romans 10:9–10 is one of the most potent passages in this regard. It reads, "You will be saved if you firmly believe that God raised Jesus from the dead and declare with your mouth, "Jesus is Lord." "Because you must confess your faith with your mouth in order to be saved, and you must believe with your heart in order to be justified."

These words unequivocally stress the significance of confessing Jesus as your Lord and believing in Him. You are saved when you profess your faith in Him and believe in Him. Salvation is mostly based on your faith in Jesus, not on your deeds or works.

I write these things to you who believe in the name of the Son of God so that you may know that you have eternal life, as the Bible also says in **1 John 5:13 Amp**. This verse is comforting and gives those who believe in Jesus a sense of assurance. You can be certain that you have Eternal Life if you put your faith in Him.

Additionally, according to **Romans 8:38–39 Amp**, "*For I am convinced [and continue to be convinced—beyond any doubt] that Neither Death, Nor Life, Nor Angels, Nor Principalities, Nor Things Present and Threatening, Nor Things to Come, Nor Powers,* [39] *Nor Height, Nor Depth, Nor Any Other Created Thing, will be able to separate us from the [Unlimited] LOVE of GOD, which is in Christ Jesus our Lord.."*

This text emphasizes how nothing can keep you from God's love after you have trusted in Jesus as your Lord and Savior. No matter what occurs in your life, you are ETERNALLY SAVED and will always be in good standing with God. Everyone who hears the gospel should be certain that they are SAVED. You are SAVED and can be sure that you have ETERNAL LIFE when you confess Jesus as your Lord and Savior. You can live with peace and security in your SALVATION since the Bible offers clear direction and assurance on this subject.

Remembering that God's Love and Grace are undeserved is also essential. He wants a relationship with you and loves you for who you are. You are already in good standing with God if you have accepted Jesus as your Lord and Savior, so there is no need to be concerned about receiving divine judgment. The passage in 1 John 4:16–18 Amp that further clarifies this concept: "As a result, we are aware of and rely on God's love for us." Gott is a synonym for love. Anyone who lives a life of love has God in them. "Love is made fully perfect among us in this way to give us confidence on the day of judgment: we resemble Jesus in this life."

This verse underlines the fact that our salvation is built on God's love. When we live in love, God and we both live in each other. This is what completes love among us and provides us the calm and assurance to face the day of judgment.

Furthermore, it is crucial to comprehend God's Love and Grace properly, since doing so will enable you to live a life that pleases Him. God's love is a reality that must be felt and demonstrated, not just a doctrine to be accepted. You will be given the ability to love people, share the gospel, and live a life that exalts God as you gain an understanding of his love.